A BOOT UP

THE SOUTH WEST COAST PATH

NORTH CORNWALL & HARTLAND

Philip Carter

First published in Great Britain in 2010

Copyright text and photographs © 2010 Philip Carter

British Library Cataloguing-in-Publication Data
A CIP record for this title is available from the British Library

ISBN 978 0 85710 014 6

PiXZ Books
Halsgrove House, Ryelands Industrial Estate,
Bagley Road, Wellington, Somerset TA21 9PZ
Tel: 01823 653777
Fax: 01823 216796
email: sales@halsgrove.com

An imprint of Halstar Ltd, part of the Halsgrove group of companies
Information on all Halsgrove titles is available at: www.halsgrove.com

Printed and bound in China by Toppan Leefung Printing Ltd

Contents

The South West Coast Path – North Cornwall & Hartland

How to use this book

The South West Coast Path offers all things to all people. For those who require a real challenge there are 630 miles (1014 km) of continuous path some of it rugged indeed. However, other parts are entirely flat and make for the easiest of walking. Whatever your choice it is hoped that this little selection will give you pleasure and maybe items of interest as well. The 'level' shown near the beginning of each walk is an indication of the exertion required. ❤ ❤ ❤ will take more effort than ❤ ❤ and ❤ ❤ than ❤ .

The waymark for the Coast Path, as it is indeed for all official long distance trails or footpaths, is a single upright acorn. So if you are in doubt as to whether you are on or off the path - look for the acorn. Having said that be careful as the National Trust use a spray of acorns as a symbol and some of the Coast Path belongs to them. Therefore you can find stretches with both. But as stated at the outset if you have a single upright acorn you are on the Coast Path.

In this series there is a selection of short, mostly circular walks, taking in parts of the Coast Path. Because they are mostly circular they can of course be walked in reverse. However, they are devised to save the best views until last so it is suggested you try them first as described. To give more opportunities of access and to vary the terrain and experience chosen walks are spread along the coast. One thing that they all have in common is a high scenic value. None of them are dull and many incorporate short stretches of the best the Coast Path has to offer.

Remember too the origin of this Coastal Path was as a walking route for revenue men patrolling to prevent smuggling. This meant that the path had to hug the coastline. The revenue men had to be able to see the end of every headland and look into each creek and inlet.

Some walks pass places of refreshment others do not. But you are always well advised to carry a flask and a little something to eat. The views are never quite so good if you are hungry!

Undoubtedly the very best time to walk is the late spring when the coastal flowers are at their best. Having said that more people walk in summer than any other time and some walks are best when the autumn colours are in evidence. Go well shod with footwear that has a grip as this will make even the hardest walk easier.

Whatever time you pick to walk and whatever area you choose you can be assured there will always be something of interest to engage the mind. The coast has for centuries been a working place and old mills, fish cellars and limekilns bear this out. The coastline too has often in times of conflict been our first line of defence so much remains to remind you of wars in the past.

These walks provide a taste of what the Coast Path has to offer. If you get hooked the best source of further information is The South West Coast Path Association. They publish an updated annual guide as well as a set of Path Descriptions covering the whole path. They are also happy to answer specific enquiries. Contact the South West Coast Path Association

(Registered Charity Number 266754)
Bowker House, Lee Mill Bridge,
Ivybridge, Devon, PL21 9EF
Telephone: 01752 896237
Fax: 01752 893654
E-mail info@swcp.org.uk
Web site www.swcp.org.uk

Introduction to North Cornwall & Hartland

This length of coast certainly can claim to have some of the most rugged and wildest scenery. The so called 'Iron Coast' is no misnomer. Yet it is not all like that, much of it offers opportunities for gentle leisure walking as you will discover if you complete all the suggested walks.

Key to Symbols Used

Level of difficulty:

Easy 🐾

Fair 🐾 🐾

More challenging 🐾 🐾 🐾

Map symbols:

🚗   Park & start

⎯⎯⎯   Tarred Road

-----   Footpath

■   Building / Town

+   Church

🍺   Pub

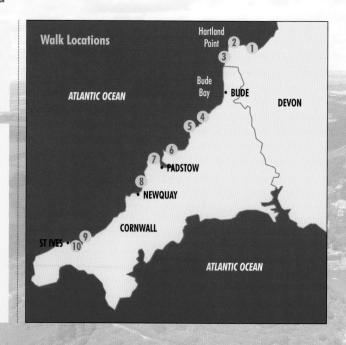

Walk Locations

Hartland Point ② ①
③

ATLANTIC OCEAN

Bude Bay ● BUDE

DEVON

⑤ ④

⑥

⑦ ● PADSTOW

⑧

● NEWQUAY

CORNWALL

ST IVES ● ⑨
⑩

ATLANTIC OCEAN

1 Clovelly - Gallantry Bower

High level spectacular bird's eye views.

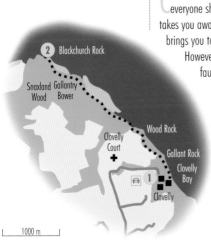

Clovelly is one of those places that everyone should visit, this walk takes you away from the crowds and brings you to an amazing viewpoint. However, this walk can be faulted on two grounds, it is not circular and there is a very steep descent which has to be climbed on the return.

Level 🐾 🐾 🐾
Length four miles (6.4 km.)
Start from the main car park at Clovelly.
OS Map Explorer 126 Clovelly & Hartland
Refreshments at the start, that is all, so take some.

Traditional Clovelly

① From the main car park go down towards the village but turn left along the road that at that point also serves as the Coast Path signed Coast Path 'Brownsham'. Then follow Coast Path signs. You soon leave the road through a high gate into a field. Follow the track forking slightly right, presently you go down steps through a rhododendron shrubbery and come up to field level again. Here look left for a view of Clovelly Court. You enter woods through a high 'deer' gate and then come to an ornate summerhouse called Angel's Wings. Later the path forks right to climb a headland, Gallantry Bower with good views. The path then descends steeply. The Coast Path is signed left inland but there is a permissive path signed 'To Viewpoint' going right – take this. Watch for little flights of stone steps on the right the first is about 75 yards and the third which you want is about 200 yards from the junction. Unsigned at time of writing. The steps lead to an arch and a surprise view of the sea that is a gem. Return through the arch and fork right down to track. You quickly pass another summerhouse designed to look inland and come to a railed headland with concrete steps above the sea. The view is your reward looking down on Blackchurch Rock and out to Lundy Island.

Clovelly, a village like a waterfall.

Blackchurch Rock from Gallantry Bower

2 Turn round and it is not quite retracing your steps because you can keep to the main path. There is not need to go back to the surprise view again unless you want to do so. When you get back to the Coast Path turn left for Clovelly and brace your self for the hill.

From Clovelly Quay

Clovelly has been well described as being like a waterfall, the houses one below another from the top of the cobbled-stepped street until they reach down to the quay. Goods are still brought down on sledges and donkeys used to carry luggage. Charles Kingsley the writer grew up here his father being the rector. • *Clovelly Court was the home of the Cary family and then the Hamlyns, London bankers, who bought the estate. The 'deer' gate is evidence of the one time deer park.* • *The impressive Blackchurch Rock is a purely natural feature. It is on the beach just seaward of Mouth Mill which is reputed to have provided some of Kingsley's inspiration for his children's novel The Water Babies.*

An aerial view of Clovelly harbour, one of the most famous villages in England.

2 Hartland Point

As good as it gets: with exhilarating coastal views.

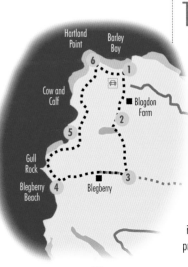

This walk takes in part of the Coast Path that some reckon is the best bit of all! At least you will be able to see why the coastline south from Hartland Point has so aptly been called the 'Iron Coast'. If that were not enough you have the opportunity to walk what is arguably the most dramatic definitive right of way in the country.

This walk though short repays the walker with splendid scenery in an isolated part of the country. Hartland pre Beeching with his considerable rail

Level 🥾🥾 not all of the route is difficult but some of it is off the beaten track.
Length three and three-quarter miles (6 km.)
Park at the car park for Hartland Point 235 275.
OS Map Explorer 126 Clovelly & Hartland
Refreshments in season at the car park but that is all, be sure you take some.

reduction programme, was renowned as the furthest place from a railway in England and this walk is beyond Hartland. Furthermore if you do not know what a 'sea capture' is you will be enlightened.

1000 m

1 Walk back out of the car park entrance and shortly when the road turns left go ahead on the bridleway sign posted 'Blegberry'. Pass the main buildings of Blagdon Farm on the left and go through field gates with bridleway waymarks down a valley.

2 Turn left at the junction with a footpath, still signed 'Blegberry' to cross a little stream. Bear right to go through a pedestrian gate along side a stream through trees and shortly cross a wooden bridge. After a few yards there is a footpath going right ignore this to proceed up a long hill. The path joins a track follow this forward until you reach a tarmac road.

Across Barley Bay to Hartland Point.

3 Here turn right and walk down the road to Blegberry Farm. Take the footpath forward between farm buildings. Follow this till it joins the Coast Path.

Parts of Blegberry Farm date back at least to the 17th century. It may in fact predate this by some four hundred years!
• *There are records of permission to fortify in Hartland for 1202 but it is not possible to be sure that this was for Blegberry.*

4 At the Coast Path turn right ascend shortly at first and then a long and scenic descent into Smoothlands valley. At the bottom those with a head for heights can extend their walk out on to Damehole Point. This distinctive headland juts out into the Atlantic but you need to cross the rocky causeway to get there. It may take some believing but this is a public footpath. Those who have

Notice that this quite large Smoothlands valley has only a miniscule stream. The reason for this is a sea capture. Streams normally wear down to sea level at their mouths. However, in a few places where the sea erodes the coastline very quickly it can cut off a stream before it reaches the sea, forming a waterfall. This is what has happened here. Titchberry Water used to flow down the valley but was cut off upstream. You will see this stream and the waterfall later in the walk.

brought their refreshment can sit on the top and look south towards Hartland Quay and have the best view there is of the 'Iron Coast'.

The way is now forward up the valley and then there is a climb back on to the ridge. At the top go forward to the corner of the field to pass through a

Titchberry Water.

pedestrian gate. Then the Coast Path turns left to descend steep steps and at the bottom crosses a bridge over Titchberry Water. When over the bridge turn left and walk towards the waterfall and the sea. There is, incidentally, a path down to the rocky shoreline if you wish to go.

Lundy lies about 12 miles of the Devon coast and is the largest island in the Bristol Channel, about three miles in length and three-quarters of a mile wide. It is a popular destination for day trippers and birdwatchers

(5) The Coast Path then swings right climbs, descends slightly then rises again to the look out above Hartland Point. Look north as you climb for a view of Lundy Island out to sea, finally do not miss the memorial stone in the corner of the last field before the look out. It is about fifteen yards after a small wooden bench seat by a footpath sign but out of sight until you are nearly upon it.

Looking north to Lundy.

Hartland Point Lighthouse.

Memorial to Glenart Castle.

6 The Coast Path descends as a concrete path behind the look out to a pedestrian gate on to the one time road to the lighthouse. As you descend concrete path look right and observe the catchment area, to your right. Unfortunately weeds are growing which disguise it but it is still obvious on close inspection (see below). It is then only a very short distance back to the car park.

Lundy Island's name derives from the Norsk for Puffin Island; evidence of unwelcome Viking raiders long ago. • The memorial stone is to the hospital ship Glenart Castle *sunk at night off the coast here by a German U-boat in 1918. Hospital ships were always clearly marked as such and fully lit at night. By normal conventions of war they were immune from attack but as defeat loomed for Germany conventions were sadly over ridden. • Hartland Point is probably the Hercules promontory of the ancient geographer Ptolemy. • The lighthouse was built by Trinity House in 1874 and blessed by Bishop Temple of Exeter formerly head-master of Repton who later became Archbishop of Canterbury. The lighthouse was automated in 1984.*

In an isolated situation such as Hartland Point mains water would not have been available. So an area of concrete was laid down to collect rainwater to provide a supply for the lighthouse and its keepers.

The rugged cliffs at Hartland Point. The lighthouse was built in 1874.

3 Hartland Quay – Speake's Mill Mouth

Rugged cliffs and plunging waterfalls.

Hartland Quay
Hotel
1
Screda Cove
Waterfall
Speake's Mill Mouth
2

1000 m

This his walk takes you to see the finest waterfall on the whole of the South West Coast Path.

The walk is only very short but it may seem longer because there is some exertion required. Unfortunately it is not circular so you have to return the

Level ❤ ❤
Length two miles (3.2 km).
Park at Hartland Quay car park 224 246
OS Map Explorer 126 Clovelly & Hartland
Refreshments at Hartland Quay.

way you came but the views up and down the coast are remarkable.

Looking back to St Catherine's Tor.

(1) From the southern end of the car park follow the Coast Path signed 'Speake's Mill'. (You can in fact go down to Hartland Quay first and start from there). The path climbs at first then descends on a stony track. The dip below and to your right is an old stream bed cut by a series of sea-captures. The most recent just before St Catherine's Tor has a small waterfall, divert to see this. You walk through flat grassland behind St Catherine's Tor. Cross the stream on stepping stones go through a meadow and ascend the other side. The path then becomes stony again and drops steeply to a little plateau beside the waterfalls at Speake's Mill Mouth.

Lower waterfalls at Speake's Mill Mouth

Main waterfalls at Speake's Mill Mouth

Hartland Quay has not only its dramatic setting but an interesting history. As the name suggests there was once a quay to make a small anchorage here. It was in existence from the reign of Elizabeth I until it was damaged in a gale in 1887 and then destroyed in another gale in 1896. It had sufficient commerce with a malt house and three lime kilns to even have its own bank which issued bank-notes. • The valley behind St Catherine's Tor was once a pool where nearby Hartland Abbey kept swans. Those were the days when swan was on the menu, cygnets the preferred eating because the old birds could be tough! The cliff alongside had a Medieval chapel dedicated to St Catherine, hence its name to this day, St Catherine's Tor.

(2) There is a path down to the beach here and to the bottom of the waterfall. Those who consider themselves mountain goats can even scramble up beside the waterfalls! They are the best falls that the Coast Path can offer; you may need to remind yourself of that as you climb back up the last hill you came down!

Sunset at Hartland Quay.

At Speake's Mill Mouth is the dramatic 50-foot plus waterfall down a rock face. When the stream levels are high enough you are rewarded with twin falls but in the summer it can just be a single fall. Look long and hard as you will not see a better waterfall anywhere on the Coast Path.

Hartland Quay.

A bird's eye view of Hartland Quay showing the car park at the start of the walk.

4 Trebarwith Strand – Tintagel Church

Walk in the Tintagel area while avoiding the crowds.

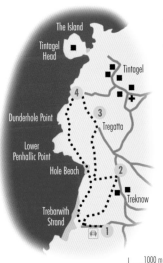

A walk through what was a busy slate extraction area but this adds interest for walkers taking this route today. While the way out is not always exciting the full reward is in the return!

This is a walk close to the tourist 'hot spot' of Tintagel but there is no need to go right in there unless you wish to do so!

1000 m

Level 🥾 🥾

Length four and a quarter miles (6.8 km).

Start Trebarwith Strand car park 054 864. There is another larger car park slightly further from the sea if the lower one is full.

OS Map Explorer 109 Bodmin Moor

Refreshments at Trebarwith Strand.

'Island' off Tintagel.

1 From the car park at Trebarwith Strand walk down towards the sea to pick up the Coast Path going North, signed 'Tintagel 2 ¼ m.'. The path climbs and there are two loop paths, the suggestion is to keep right on both. Shortly after the second loop there is a footpath going right towards Treknow take this. At the unsigned junction keep right. The grass path becomes a track and joins another north of Treknow. Bear left on this second track and ignore the first path going left but proceed a little distance up the road to turn left on another footpath signed 'To the Coast Path'.

2 Follow this sunken and sometimes soggy path to a junction with the Coast Path again. At

Looking inland over Trebarwith Strand.

Trebarwith in a gale is an impressive sight and at high tide there will be little to see of the Strand part of the full name. However, on a calm day when the tide is out there is a mile long beach. It was an exporting port for the local slate; this despite the difficult task in days of sail for boats to manoeuvre around Gull Rock. The awkwardness of access led to shipwrecks. The sloop Jane from Boscastle came to grief in 1844, the Resolution from Padstow in 1888 and despite its optimistic name The Narrow Escape from Clovelly was also wrecked here.

certain times of the year the banks are colourful with garden escapees Red Hot Pokers and Montbretia. Turn right and follow the Coast Path North for a short while. You cross a stone stile and shortly there is a path going right for Tregatta, ignore this. Very soon another path goes off right and forward for Trevillick, take this. In the first two fields the line is straight but in the third it goes at an angle to reach the exit. The path is then a track again curving around the farm.

3 At the junction turn sharp left, ignoring a later left turn, to go to Tintagel Church.

The church dedicated to St Materiana is one of the oldest in Cornwall. There is a double Cornish stile at the entrance gate, have a look at this they are nearly as scarce as hen's teeth on the Coast Path. One can conjecture that they were the inspiration for the modern cattle grid. The saddest memorial in the churchyard is perhaps that to the fourteen-year old Italian

Cornish stile at Tintagel Church.

Churchyard grave of Iota's cabin boy.

cabin boy Domenico Catanese. He was drowned when the vessel the *Iota* foundered in a blizzard off Lye Rock near Tintagel in 1893, although all the rest of the crew survived. A wooden cross and a life belt, that might have saved him, marks his grave

4 From Tintagel Church follow the track across to meet the Coast Path, there is no sign but a small metal cycle rack marks the start.

When you reach the Coast turn left. Shortly there are some concrete foundations. Stop here and turn round for your best view of The Island on which Tintagel Castle was built. There are good views forward to Gull Rock off Trebarwith and well down the North Cornish coast. You pass the Youth Hostel in its dramatic setting on Glebe Cliff and then walk the improved path around the two Penhallic Points. The path follows the coast past old slate quarries; there is a particularly spectacular one at Hole Beach. When you get to the two loops again, keep right for the better view. Back in Trebarwith Strand turn inland to the car park.

Lye Rock where Iota was wrecked.

The site of Tintagel Castle on its 'island' was once a Celtic monastery. Later the castle was built but apparently never saw a shot fired in anger. It did however serve as a prison, once holding Warwick the Kingmaker. The Youth hostel was part of the quarrying complex. 'Glebe' tells us that this was once church land usually for the benefit of the local incumbent. Either he might cultivate it himself or simply lease it and accept rentals. Evidence of one time slate quarrying is very apparent, a huge rock pillar has been

Gull Rock off Trebarwith Strand.

often dictated by the tides perhaps with a start at four in the morning. Unsociable hours indeed! Before descending look inland to where there were more slate quarries. One has a ruined engine house, while most engine houses in Cornwall were at mines; here was one for a quarry.

Old quarry at Hole Beach.

left in the quarry near Hole Beach. Various theories have been offered for this but the most likely one is that it was left as a support for a derrick. Some of these quarries were worked within living memory and incredibly hard work it was too. Shifts were

Tintagel. One of the most enigmatic historic sites in the country.

5 Port Isaac – Port Quin

Undulating but a walk full of interest.

This walk takes an inland route from Port Isaac to Port Quin and then returns by the Coast Path. It will be surprising if you do not enjoy the return more than the outward journey. If you want to put the mind to something imponderable, consider this. Cornwall County Council spent a lot of time and money obstructing the coastal route which they could have had for free! Then having lost the public enquiry, possibly to show their pique, erected an enormous ugly fence along the route which was soon nicknamed 'Hadrian's Fence'.

Level 🦋🦋🦋 although the cliffs here do not rise above 250 feet there is a remarkable amount of climbing. Anyone with an aversion to steps should leave this walk out!

Length just under six miles (9.6 km)

Start at the main car park above and to the east of Port Isaac 999 810. You used to be able to park on the Harbour Beach, which shortened the walk a little but it could increase the stress level because being a beach it is subject to the tide!

OS Map Explorer 106 Newquay & Padstow

Refreshments plenty in Port Isaac but none elsewhere.

Kellan Head

Greengarden Cove

5

Varley Head

Lobber Point

Downgate Cove

Port Quin

3

4

Port Isaac

1

2

🚗

1000 m

Port Isaac

This stretch of the north Cornwall coast is not as dramatic as some others but is none the less rewarding. It can certainly not be accomplished without effort.

Port Gaverne so peaceful now was once a busy port exporting slate. Port Isaac's name may come from the Cornish word 'isic' meaning corn. The place entered the national news a few years ago when a Land Rover went through the roof of one of the houses! More recently it has featured in the television series Doc Martin as Port Wenn.

1 From the car park descend to the Coast Path and turn left to circumvent the little headland which separates Port Gaverne from Port Isaac. Be sure to look right, north-easterly,

along the coast there are good views as far as Tintagel. The Coast path joins the road going down to the village. Pass round the back of the harbour.

2 The way is then up Roscarrock Hill, just past the last house

Beach parking, Port Isaac.

on the right is a footpath leading off left, sign posted 'Port Quin inland route', take this. (If you reach a cul-de-sac with the Coast Path signed right you have missed the path you want, retrace your steps.) At first the path confined between two banks goes steeply upwards then after a stone stile runs along the side of an open field to reach a second stone stile. This is a footpath junction.

(3) The way you want is straight forward but at the time of writing there is no trace of a path on the ground. All you can do is to walk forward keeping the same distance parallel to the hedge bank a little below you to your right. Presently you will come across a worn path going diagonally left; this is the path you need. It leads towards a field gate but the path is sign posted right just

before you reach the gate. The path descends steeply to a bridge, follow the path forward signed 'Port Quin'. The path then climbs sharply to a stile that goes slightly right to follow the field boundary.

Presently just before Roscarrock Farm the path takes a right angled turn right and proceeds along a broad track for just over a mile. There are three stiles and gates, at the third whilst the track then sweeps away up to the right the path you want is ahead and downhill into the valley. You come to a final field gate and pass down a grass path in front of Varley Cottage to join the road. Go forward along this but just before the first slight bend look for the remnants of ruined cottages to the right of the road, of which more anon.

Doyden Point.

(4) In Port Quin note on the left the one time fish cellars now National Trust holiday lets. Turn right on the Coast Path up steps to bear left and shortly look left to see the little tower on Doyden Point. The path then goes round Kellan Head, makes a fair imitation of a switchback and passes two coves before cutting across the neck of Varley Head.

Fake front door for Amy Foster.

Roscarrock has been settled for a many years, parts of it date back to medieval times. • Port Quin was undoubtedly of more importance once than it is now, hence the abandoned cottages. It is possible that the rise of Port Isaac led to the decline of Port Quin. Certainly, there appears to be no basis for two local legends of depopulation. One concerned a disaster at sea caused by fishing on the Sabbath; the other the activities of the press gang which led to the loss of the men folk and the evacuation of the village. • Much of the filming of Joseph Conrad's Amy Foster took place here. A fake shop doorway was built across the Coast Path and the galvanized roofed building by the one time harbour became a blacksmith's forge where horses were shod on the film set.

The tower on Doyden Point was built about 1830 and was reputed to have been used for wild parties, though it must be said, it looks an unlikely position for such activities! Today it is a holiday let.

(5) The Coast Path then descends steeply to Pine Haven crosses a bridge and climbs up again on a track to go round Lobber Point bringing Port Isaac into sight. As you round the headland the path across the grass seems to be leaving the coast but this is right in this instance.

Making footpaths the modern way, near Port Quin.

Descend in front of a terrace of houses to return to the road just a little above where you originally left it. Retrace your steps behind the harbour up the hill and round the headland to regain the car park.

Port Quin, fish cellars before conversion.

Port Isaac looking its best on a sunny day.

6 New Polzeath · Pentire Point

Offers the walker Cornwall's best all round viewpoint.

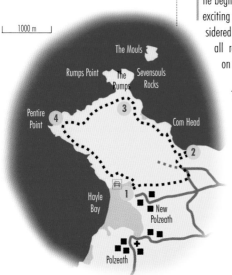

The beginning of the walk is not exciting but Pentire Point is considered by some to have the best all round views of anywhere on the coast in Cornwall.

The walk starts up an inland valley, goes along a minor road through an old mining area to get out on the coast. It is then coastal all the way back to New Polzeath.

Level 🍂 🍂
Length just over four miles (6.4 km)
Park if you can on the seafront at New Polzeath 935 795, there is another large pay and display car park just inland.
OS Map Explorer 106 Newquay & Padstow
Refreshments sporadic at New Polzeath but plenty at nearby Polzeath itself.

View of Pentire Point across the Camel.

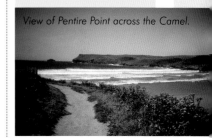

37

From the seafront car park walk back around the corner of the road to a Coast Path sign that says 'New Polzeath' one way and 'Port Quin' etc the other, take neither but go along the track with dwellings on the right which has a little notice 'Pentireglaze Haven', soon where track swings left, go forward on the bridleway through a series of farm gates. On reaching a minor road turn left to go down in a dip and up the other side, then left again signed 'Pentire Farm and Lead Mine' car park. As you go through a gate you look forward across the mouth of the Camel to Stepper Point with its day-mark and beyond to Trevose Head with its lighthouse. Enter the car park which soon appears on your right. In the park by the information board a

View up the Camel to Brea Hill.

path goes right over the old lead mine spoil heaps. Bear slightly right to

cross a field area to reach the Coast Path by an old stone stile.

There was a long history, nearly four centuries, of intermittent lead mining at Pentireglaze but production ceased in about the middle of the nineteenth century.

However, afterwards passing inland of The Rumps headland you presently pass a path turning inland to Pentire Farm shortly on the Coast Path you go through a pedestrian gate. Then in a dip on the left is a massive slate stone seat. Next comes a little steep ascent. Coastal walkers would hardly call it a hill! As this levels off on the right is a seat and beyond it the plaque magnificently positioned above the sea.

Laurence Binyon memorial.

(2) Turn left on to the Coast Path. Soon there are good views back along north coast to Tintagel Island and beyond.

(3) Pass behind The Rumps to get to Pentire Point. You can of course divert on to The Rumps to get a view of the bird inhabited offshore islet The Mouls, but this will add a little to your mileage. It is easy to miss the Lawrence Binyon plaque, as this writer did the first time!

The Rumps from Pentire Point.

The Rumps was another of the Iron Age cliff castles that are sometimes found on the Cornish coast. It had three ramparts and just one entrance. • During World War I Lawrence Binyon was inspired by this coastline to write his most famous poem To the Fallen "They shall not grow old, as we that are left grow old; Age shall not weary them, nor the years condemn".

View from the Binyon memorial to The Rumps.

downhill but with a couple of short climbs towards the end just to remind you, you are after all walking the Coast Path!

(4) At Pentire pause, as well as views along the coast you can see well up the estuary of the River Camel and much of the surrounding countryside. Then follow Coast Path back to New Polzeath it is mainly

There were plans just prior to World War II for Pentire Point to become a building development. Happily there was sufficient opposition to raise funds for its purchase and present it to the National Trust. • The River Camel rises on Bodmin moor and is about thirty miles in length. Perhaps disappointingly its name has nothing to do with the animal. It derives from old Cornish for crooked, a reference to its convoluted course.

The headland at Pentire along which much of Walk 6 is taken, affording spectacular views up and down the coast.

7 Trevone - Stepper Point

A walk taking in estuary and coast.

The scenery is impressive but the round holes and interesting rock formations add much to the whole experience.

An intriguing yet contrasting foil to a walk round Pentire on the other side of the mouth of the River Camel.

Level 💜 💜
Length six miles (9.6 km.)
Start Trevone car park 892 752
OS Map Explorer 106 Newquay & Padstow
Refreshments at Trevone and with a diversion at Lellizzick Farm part way round.

Hawker's Cove.

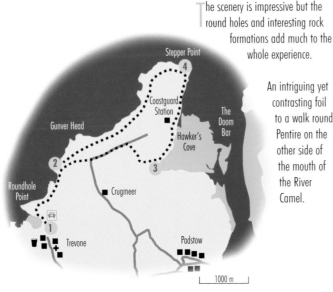

Stepper Point
4
Coastguard Station
Gunver Head
Hawker's Cove
The Doom Bar
3
2
Roundhole Point
Crugmeer
1
Trevone
Padstow

1000 m

43

Round Hole at Trevone.

(1) Walk out of the back of the car park to the road behind the beach here pick up the Coast Path going eastwards signed 'Hawker's Cove'. You climb steps walk through a short piece of grassland and cross a stone stile. Immediately after the stile are two paths going right, the first at about an angle of 'eleven o'clock' the second at 'ten o'clock'. It is the second you want to take you directly to the Round Hole. You can then proceed up the hill to rejoin the Coast Path. At the top of this rise there is a 'ruin' on the right. Just after this turn left off the path to get a better look of the natural 'bridge', as it is called at Porthmissen.

After this little diversion rejoin the Coast Path which presently goes down in a dip. Here there is a small stream on each side of a stile in a hedge bank. The path rises again and descends into a second small valley.

Trevone has all the facilities but being largely of modern origin has little of interest. • The round holes were originally just caves but then the roof has fallen in. Some people find it difficult to envisage that all the material that filled the hole has passed out to sea through the narrow outlet below. However, that is exactly what has happened. • Porthmissen Bridge as it is called is a spectacular natural multi-arch made up of contrasting rock strata. The person who said it reminded him of a giant humbug must have been hungry indeed!

Natural arches at Porthmissen Bridge.

2 Turn inland on a path just across the stream. This gets less defined as you climb but keep close to the dip caused by the stream. At the top you will find you had been on a permissive path. It joins a minor road at a right angle. Go left. In about half a mile another permissive path, also signed as a car park, leads off and downhill on the right, take this. At the bottom far corner is a gate with a track going on further down. This track swings left opposite a small wooden bridge. Here look for an inconspicuous opening on the left signed 'Coast Path'.

3 Go up steps turn right and presently come out just above a beach of the Camel Estuary. As you reach the estuary the first two fields were the site of an ancient trading settlement. 'Time Team' the archaeological programme on Channel 4 carried out an excavation here. Look across the Doom Bar to the rounded Brea Hill on the other side. Go forwards towards the sea to Hawker's Cove. After the first building, the one time life-boat house there is a stile and

The old concrete buildings up on the right as you climb the stream valley near Crugmeer were used during World War II for an airfield. More surprisingly there was also a Royal Naval Air Station there in World War I but accommodation then was canvas hangers and wooden huts.

then a footpath junction, go left. At the next junction right on the road, dip a little and turn right off the road past a garden. Go up some steps and shortly come to some more going up on to a road, take these and turn right to presently continue on the Coast Path. There is a long climb to reach Stepper Point with its views across Padstow Bay to Pentire Point and the islet of Newland off shore.

Padstow has had a lifeboat for 140 years and it was here at Hawker's Cove until 1967 when it was moved to a better site on the east side of Trevose Head. Over the years the crews achieved a splendid record of saving over four hundred lives. The Coastguard Cottages remind us of the origins of the Coast Path when it was regularly

Looking towards Stepper Point.

patrolled on foot. The second row of cottages were to accommodate the pilots who guided the vessels in and out of the estuary. Despite the Doom Bar, Padstow was for centuries a busy port, natural harbours being scarce on the

North Cornish coast. Much commerce came in and went out of the port and many thousands of emigrants sailed from Padstow looking to start a new life overseas.

The most incredible fact established by 'Time Team' was the long length of occupation of the ancient settlement, over two thousand years from the Bronze Age to post-Roman Dark Ages. It was a trading community as evinced by pottery from North Africa and modern Greece and Turkey then the Byzantine Empire. Presumably tin and copper were exported in return, metallic slag was found on site as well as domestic goods such as spindle whorls. • The notorious Doom Bar has over the years seen the end of several hundred ships including three lifeboats on its treacherous sands. In one sad month at the end of the nineteenth century two lifeboats were lost and eight crewmen drowned.

(4) The Coast Path now bears west passing close to the large daymark. Another islet Gulland is seen ahead; a footpath leads off inland but ignore it, stay with the Coast Path. This is a fine stretch of high level walking by Pepper and Butter Holes. The path is slightly inland behind Gunver Head and the distinctive Middle Merope Island is on your right. Soon you are back to where you turned inland but this time just stay with the Coast Path all the way to walk the little bit you missed near the start when you went to see the Round Hole. You are soon back to Trevone.

The daymark on Stepper Point is forty feet high and was built in an effort to reduce the loss of life on the Doom Bar. Capstans were also erected on the point to winch in vessels.

Daymark on Stepper Point.

A superb view from Padstow (foreground) along the length of the headland to Stepper Point. The photograph includes much of the area covered by Walk 7.

8 Mawgan Porth – Bedruthan Steps

A quiet stretch between two tourist hot spots.

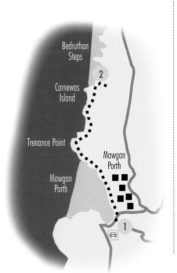

This walk takes you to see Bedruthan Steps, a place that is justifiably well known as one of the great views in a very scenic county. However, as it is so well known, do not expect to enjoy it alone.

This walk is 'there and back' not circular, however if you do not turn round too often on your way out you may be well pleased with the views on your return.

Level 🐾 but there is one long climb
Length just over four miles (6.4 km.)
Start at Mawgan Porth car park 850 672
OS Map Explorer 106 Newquay & Padstow
Refreshments at both ends; at Mawgan Porth and for a long season from February until November at National Trust Carnewas near Bedruthan Steps.

1000 m

① From the car park cross the road to the entrance of the beach. The Coast Path is sign posted 'Porthcothan via Bedruthan' and goes along the beach for a short while passing the lifeguard's lookout hut. It then goes up steps, climbs for a while and, dips to a stream to climb again up on to Trenance Point. As you ascend, just before passing a large bungalow is a shallow dip that has a shed and a green house in it. This, though it is hard to believe was once a canal. Continue northward, following the Coast Path until you come to Bedruthan Steps the chain of rocky islets.

Trenance Point from Mawgan Porth.

Bedruthan Steps.

Porth is the Cornish word for 'cove' so Mawgan Porth is the cove, of the much less visited St Mawgan a little way inland.

• *The canal on Trenance Point which is now an inconspicuous ditch was intended to link in a semi-circular route Mawgan Porth, via St Columb Major and Minor, with St Columb Porth, near Newquay further down the coast. Authorised in 1773, construction work went on from 1775 to 1779, but it was never completed. Both ends were to have inclined planes to bring goods to and from ships.*

(2) The nearest building is the National Trust Carnewas that usually offers refreshment. Then fortified return the way you came. If the tide is out, when you get to the stream you can descend the steps and walk back along the beach so avoiding the last little rise.

Bedruthan Steps probably originally applied to the actual steps that went down to the beach. However the name has been transposed to refer to the string of islets just off shore. A relatively modern legend of a giant Bedruthan who used the rocky islets as stepping stones then began to circulate. Thankfully, you do not have to believe this unlikely tale to admire them. More factually one of the islets is called Samaritan Island. This is after the wreck of the brig the *Good Samaritan* in 1846. She had a rich and portable cargo that was too tempting for the locals so that a number of them finished up in Bodmin gaol!

Sea Holly can be seen nearby.

St Columb Canal on Trenance Point.

Bedruthan Steps in rough seas.

9 Godrevy – Navax Point

A scenic walk with close-up views of Godrevy Island.

A short but scenic walk that gives you a good close view of Godrevy lighthouse on its island and distant views along the coast.

An easy and simple walk with only one small climb. If you take binoculars you might have fun watching the colony of thirty or more grey seals that are resident on Godrevy Island.

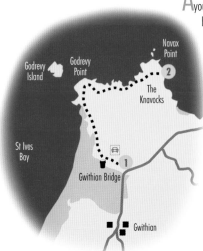

Level 🏔

Length just over three and a half miles (5.6 km.)

Park at the National Trust Godrevy car park 586 422 (There is another car park further on but that will shorten your walk.)

OS Map Explorer 102 Land's End

Refreshments there is a pub just before the car park and a café alongside it.

The placename Navax comes from the Cornish 'kynyavos' meaning 'autumn farm'

1000 m

55

Godrevy Island from The Knavocks.

1 Walk a few yards along the road that continues from the car park and then go left and forward to pick up the Coast Path unmarked at first but well worn. You can then walk out to Godrevy Point with its splendid views of Godrevy Island. From there continue to Navax Point going just beyond the old trig point now with the National Trust cairn to look north along the coast.

On Godrevy Head is an earth bank which may have been erected when there was the threat of the Spanish Armada in 1588. Godrevy Lighthouse was built by Trinity House in 1859 in answer to a public outcry of ships lost there. It was not only the island itself that was the hazard; a reef called the Stones extends westwards adding to the danger. One of the last ships to go aground there pre-lighthouse, was the steamer *Nile* that was lost with all hands in 1854. Going back in history a wreck that made the news was of the ship carrying royal possessions that went aground on the day in 1649 when King Charles I was executed. Virginia Woolf spent time in St Ives and Godrevy lighthouse was the inspiration for her book *To the Lighthouse*. The lighthouse was converted to solar power in 1993.

2 Then turn around to return the way you came, surprising how different some of the views are. There is an obvious short cut back omitting Godrevy Head if you want to take it. It is a particularly rewarding walk in spring when so many flowers are out.

Seals are often to be seen off Navax Point and a colony inhabit Godrevy.

Godrevy Island and lighthouse.

Just about the whole of Walk 9 is contained in this aerial photograph.
Godrevy headland lies in the foreground with Navax Point beyond.

10 Lelant - St Ives

A charming walk near to the town.

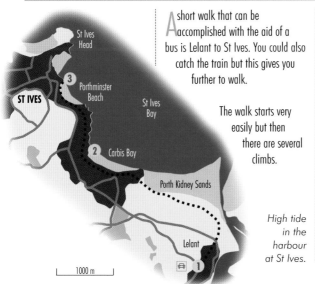

A short walk that can be accomplished with the aid of a bus is Lelant to St Ives. You could also catch the train but this gives you further to walk.

The walk starts very easily but then there are several climbs.

St Ives Head

③ Porthminster Beach

ST IVES

St Ives Bay

② Carbis Bay

Porth Kidney Sands

Lelant

High tide in the harbour at St Ives.

1000 m

Level 🌿 🌿

Length three and a half miles (5.6 km.)

Start by catching the bus from the bus station at St Ives. There is a large car park close by.

OS Maps Explorer 102 Land's End

Refreshments plenty in St Ives, a pub in Lelant, and variable according to season, both at Carbis Bay and right at the end at Porthminster Beach.

1 Catch the bus at St Ives and get off in the main street of Lelant just before the Post Office.

2 Walk back to the corner and take the road sign posted 'Golf Course and St Uny Church'. Go along this road to the church where the Coast Path leaves the road The

Overlooking St Ives.

Coast Path goes down and under the railway line before turning left. Then follow the Coast Path to Carbis Bay.

St Ives, as well as being a fishing port was also a mining town, for both tin and copper. Even some of the radium used by Marie Curie for her experiments came from here. •
An art colony grew up from the end of the nineteenth century. Today, of course, St Ives is chiefly known as a holiday resort, its debt to the Great Western Railway that promoted it as the 'Naples of the West' largely forgotten. • The writer Rosamund Pincher was born in St Ives. • The area between St Ives and Lelant was once used for flower growing. It was an eye catching sight to see a whole field of vibrantly coloured anemones in flower.

Parking problem St Ives.

The church at Lelant is interesting on two counts. The gateway that you pass is made from foundry slag from the days when copper was smelted at Hayle. Later the local ore was taken to Swansea in South Wales for processing. This proving more economical than having to bring in large quantities of coal. Inside the church is a big monument for the Praed family. They went to London, made good, and gave their name to Praed Street outside Paddington Station.
  • There used to be a passenger ferry across the narrows from Hayle to the Lelant shore but this ceased operation about the beginning of World War II. There was a brief revival later but it did not last long.

Gateway at Lelant Church.

Praed family monument in Lelant Church.

A classic view over St Ives.

(3) Continue with the Coast Path from Carbis Bay later past the Baulking House down to Porthminster and very shortly St Ives. There are a few unmarked paths leading down to beaches but the Coast Path is usually obvious. If you want to get back to the bus starting point turn left up the steps opposite the Pedn Olva Hotel.

Overlooking St Uny Church and the golf course at Lelant, with the view towards Hayle.

Baulking House at St Ives.

THE BAULKING HOUSE
A Huer's Lookout from which watch was kept for shoals of pilchards in the bay and the movements of the seine boats were directed

The Baulking House was a huer's look out station. In the days when pilchards were plentiful their presence could be detected by changes in the sea's colouration. Watchers, the huers, would look out for shoals, alert the local fishermen and indicate where they should go. Hue here has the same root as in 'hue and cry' the one time pursuit of criminals. St Ives was one of the great pilchard fishing towns of Cornwall, enormous quantities being landed here. The local museum has stencils once used in the export trade, such as for Ancona, Bari, and Leghorn that show the extent of the trade.

Porthminster Beach where the walk ends.